NATURAL WONDERS OF THE WORLD

THE AMAZON RAINFOREST

by Rebecca Kraft Rector

FOCUS READERS

FOCUS READERS

WWW.FOCUSREADERS.COM

Focus Readers is distributed by North Star Editions:
sales@northstareditions.com | 888-417-0195

Produced for Focus Readers by Red Line Editorial.

Content Consultant: Brian J. Godfrey, PhD, Department of Earth Science and Geography, Vassar College

Photographs ©: apomares/iStockphoto, cover, 1; Dr Morley Read/Shutterstock Images, 4–5; Red Line Editorial, 6; DouglasOlivares/iStockphoto, 9; JohnnyLye/iStockphoto, 10–11; PCostaBaldi/iStockphoto, 13; Anita SKV/Shutterstock Images, 15; salparadis/iStockphoto, 16–17; Claudiio Doenitz/iStockphoto, 19; SaveJungle/Shutterstock Images, 21; TinaFields/iStockphoto, 22–23; filipefrazao/iStockphoto, 24–25; Marcelo Horn/iStockphoto, 27; KalypsoWorldPhotography/Shutterstock Images, 29

ISBN
978-1-63517-511-0 (hardcover)
978-1-63517-583-7 (paperback)
978-1-63517-727-5 (ebook pdf)
978-1-63517-655-1 (hosted ebook)

Library of Congress Control Number: 2017948092

Printed in the United States of America
Mankato, MN
November, 2017

ABOUT THE AUTHOR

Rebecca Kraft Rector is a writer, librarian, and researcher. She is the author of novels, nonfiction books, and more than 100 nonfiction articles.

TABLE OF CONTENTS

CHAPTER 1

A FOREST FULL OF LIFE

A warm rain is falling in the Amazon rainforest. The tall trees and plants grow close together. This vegetation slows down the raindrops. Some drops take more than 10 minutes to reach the ground. They must travel down as far as 150 feet (46 m) through the leaves.

The Amazon rainforest is filled with giant trees.

The Amazon takes up much of northwest Brazil.

Amazonia is a huge region with many different types of areas. These include everything from swamps to grasslands. But the region is best known for containing the world's largest tropical rainforest. It covers more than 2 million square miles (5.2 million sq km). Most of the Amazon is in Brazil. But it also spreads into eight other countries.

Like all rainforests, the Amazon is an area of tall trees and plenty of rain. Approximately 120 inches (305 cm) of rain falls every year. The Amazon is generally warm and humid. Temperatures remain around 78 to 82 degrees Fahrenheit (26 to 28°C).

The Amazon rainforest is full of life from the treetops to the forest floor. Millions of different kinds of plants and animals live there.

Many of these plants and animals can be found nowhere else on Earth. No one knows how many **species** live in the Amazon. Scientists are still trying to count and identify them. Native people have long lived in the Amazon, too.

The Amazon River runs through the rainforest. It is one of the longest rivers in the world. Water flows from the Andes Mountains in the west, and from forest floors of regional rainforests, into the river. This means the rainforest is a **river basin**. It is the largest river basin in the world. Amazonia makes up the area that includes the rainforest, the river basin, and the river.

Depending on how it's measured, the Amazon River is either the longest or second-longest in the world.

CHAPTER 2

FORMING THE AMAZON

Millions of years ago, the Amazon River flowed west. Then the Andes Mountains rose up and blocked the river. This made a huge lake. After about five million years, the water broke through to the east. The Amazon River flowed again, but in the opposite direction. The river drained the lake and left behind wetlands.

The Amazon River has existed in some form for millions of years.

Scientific experts differ on the natural history of the Amazon basin. Most agree that the rainforest gradually developed over millions of years. Similarly, most agree that plant life in the area has changed significantly in the last few thousand years.

The level of water in the oceans dropped during the most recent ice age. This happened between 2.6 million and 11,700 years ago. The drop in water level made the Amazon rainforest drier. Some scientists think savannas took over the area. Other scientists believe the rainforest still covered a smaller area. However, they do not think the savannas

Leopoldo Lake is in the Venezuelan Amazon.

took over completely. When the ice age ended, the rainforest grew again.

Many plants and animals thrived in the rainforest. The Amazon has harsh conditions for humans. But native Tupí-Guaraní groups have lived in the rainforest for thousands of years.

At one point, millions of people might have lived in Amazonia. However, European settlers arrived in the 1500s. After that, new diseases, forced labor, and regional warfare greatly reduced the native populations.

MAKING MOUNTAINS

How did the Andes rise up to block the Amazon River? Earth's surface is made up of huge plates. These plates move very slowly across a layer of melted rock. When these plates collide, they can create earthquakes and volcanic eruptions. They can also create mountains. Millions of years ago, two plates collided in South America. The edges of the plates were forced upward. The edges rose to form the Andes mountain range.

The Andes Mountains mark the southwestern edge of the Amazon region.

CHAPTER 3

PLANTS AND ANIMALS

The Amazon rainforest contains approximately 30 percent of Earth's plant and animal species. Each layer of the forest provides a unique **habitat**. The emergent layer is on top. Trees such as Brazil nut and kapok grow there. They are exposed to wind, sun, and rain. Leaves are small and waxy to keep in moisture.

The emergent layer gets the most direct sunlight.

Treetops in the emergent layer are not strong, so most creatures that live there fly or glide. Bats, birds, and butterflies live in this layer. So does the harpy eagle.

Below the emergent layer is the canopy. Almost two-thirds of rainforest plants and animals live here. Leafy branches make

NEW DISCOVERIES

New creatures and plants are still being discovered in the Amazon rainforest. Between 2010 and 2013, more than 400 new species were discovered. Of these discoveries, 258 were plants. Other discoveries included a tiny frog the size of a thumb and a piranha that does not eat meat. A monkey that purrs was another.

Howler monkeys live in the canopy layer of the rainforest.

a roof that keeps out most of the sun, wind, and rain. Leaves are smooth, shiny, and pointed so that water can roll off. Blossoms and fruit grow throughout the year. Canopy plants include **epiphytes** and fig trees. Among the animals in the canopy are monkeys, parrots, and sloths. There are more insects than any other creature in the canopy. Some of the insects include beetles, bees, and ants.

The understory layer is dim and humid. Plants include short trees, orchids, and shrubs. Leaves are large and dark green. Flowers are large and pale. Animals such as salamanders, tree frogs, and tree snakes live in this layer. So do many birds and insects.

The bottom layer is the forest floor. It is dark, wet, and still. Fungi and the roots of many plants are here. Giant armadillos use their front claws to dig for insects such as termites, ants, and millipedes. Scorpions, iguanas, and poison dart frogs live here as well. The jaguar and the capybara roam the forest floor. The capybara is the world's largest rodent.

LAYERS OF THE RAINFOREST

The Amazon rainforest has four layers. Each layer is home to different plants and animals.

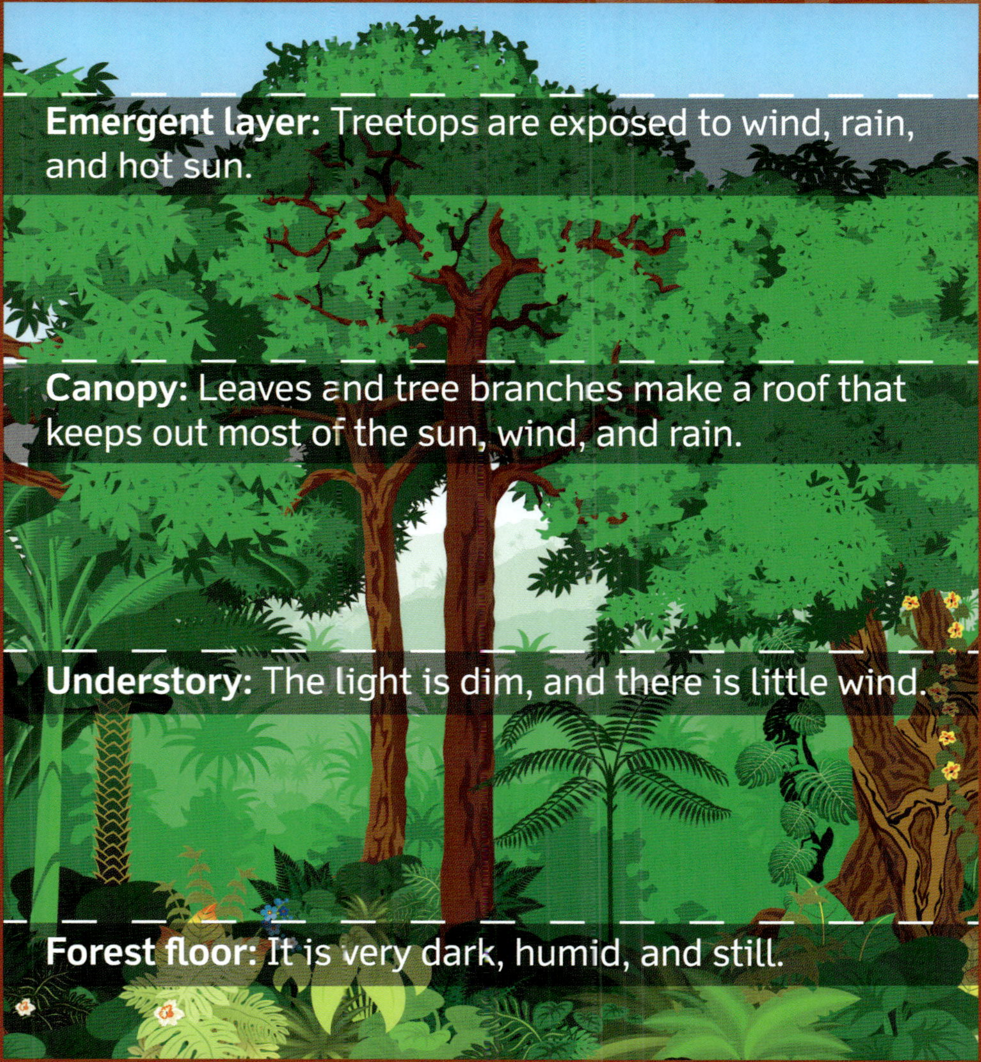

BRAZIL NUT

The Brazil nut tree is one of the tallest in the Amazon rainforest. Some reach 200 feet (61 m) high. Its seeds are hidden inside a large fruit that weighs 5 pounds (2.3 kg). When the fruit falls from the tall trees, it can race downward at speeds of up to 50 miles per hour (80 km/h). The fruit often makes a small crater when it lands.

The agouti is the only known animal with teeth sharp enough to open the hard fruit. This rodent eats some of the seeds, or nuts, and buries the rest. Some of these nuts sprout and form new trees. The Brazil nut tree needs the agouti to survive. Laws in Brazil are intended to protect Brazil nut trees. However, widespread **deforestation** threatens the trees' survival.

Brazil nuts are not actually nuts. They're seeds.

CHAPTER 4

THE AMAZON RAINFOREST TODAY

The Amazon rainforest is an important part of planet Earth. It produces oxygen and absorbs carbon dioxide in the atmosphere, while also stabilizing the climate. More plants and animals live in the rainforest than anywhere else in the world. In addition, more than 100 groups of native people make their homes there.

The Amazon rainforest is often called "the lungs of our planet."

Useful products come from the Amazon rainforest. Rubber trees produce natural rubber. This has long proved essential for **industrial** production. Woods, spices, fruits, and coffee are a few everyday products from the rainforest. Many medicines come from rainforests, too. Only a tiny number of species have been examined for helpful qualities. Many more life-saving medicines may yet be found.

However, the Amazon rainforest is under threat from people cutting or burning the forest. This is called deforestation. Nearly 20 percent of the Amazon rainforest has been destroyed since 1970. Trees are being cut down to

Timber from the Amazon rainforest is very valuable.

make room for pastures, farms, and dams. Trees are also cut for logging and mining.

The growth of large and small cities has transformed large parts of the region. At least 30 million people now live there. This increasing human impact destroys natural habitats. It might cause species to become extinct.

Governments and **conservation** groups are trying to help the rainforest. Farmers and businesses are being encouraged to use **sustainable** practices. This means they will try to save resources and be thoughtful in their choices. For instance,

SAVE THE RAINFOREST!

There are many things you can do to help our planet.

1. Learn about the rainforest and share what you learn.
2. Join a group that helps save rainforests.
3. Start at home by protecting plants and animals in your neighborhood.
4. Recycle and use sustainable products.
5. Ask where products came from. It is usually illegal to take plants or animals from the wild.

Visitors explore the Cuyabero River in Ecuador.

if trees must be cut, then young trees are spared or new trees are planted.

Brazil has created a network of parks in the Amazon. These are protected areas. Sustainable **tourism** is a way for businesses and farmers to make money without destroying the rainforest.

FOCUS ON
THE AMAZON RAINFOREST

Write your answers on a separate piece of paper.

1. Write a letter to a friend describing how the Amazon rainforest was formed.

2. Would you like to live in the rainforest canopy? Why or why not?

3. In which layer do most creatures fly or glide?

A. understory
B. emergent
C. canopy

4. How would the destruction of the rainforest affect the discovery of new medicines?

A. Plants that might have helpful qualities will be lost forever.
B. Plants that might have helpful qualities will get confused for other plants.
C. Plants that might have helpful qualities will have more room to grow.

Answer key on page 32.

GLOSSARY

conservation
The careful protection of plants, animals, and natural resources so they are not lost or wasted.

deforestation
The removal of the trees in a forest, usually by cutting or burning.

epiphytes
Plants that grow on other plants but do not harm them.

habitat
The type of place where plants or animals normally grow or live.

industrial
Related to the production of goods in a factory.

river basin
An area of land from which water drains into a river.

species
A group of animals or plants that are similar.

sustainable
Having to do with methods that do not harm or use up a resource.

tourism
When people visit an area for recreation.

TO LEARN MORE

BOOKS

Clarke, Ginjer L. *What's Up in the Amazon Rainforest*. New York: Grosset & Dunlap, 2015.

Jackson, Tom. *The Amazon*. New York: DK, 2015.

The Mysteries of the Amazon Rain Forest. Chicago: World Book, 2015.

WEBSITES

Visit **www.focusreaders.com** to find lesson plans, activities, links, and other resources related to this title.

INDEX

Answer Key: 1. Answers will vary; **2.** Answers will vary; **3.** B; **4.** A